Galway in Old Photographs

Peadar O'Dowd

GILL & MACMILLAN

Gill & Macmillan Ltd
Hume Avenue
Park West
Dublin 12
with associated companies throughout the world
www.gillmacmillan.ie

© 2003 Peadar O'Dowd
0 7171 3483 0
Design and print origination by O'K Graphic Design, Dublin
Printed by ColourBooks Ltd, Dubin

The paper used in this book is made from the wood pulp of managed forests.
For every tree felled, at least one tree is planted, thereby renewing natural resources.

A catalogue record is available for this book from the British Library.

3 5 4 2

Contents

Introduction

L ittle apples are not the only items God created to prove He exists. Once formed, they grow into bigger fruit, thus underlining another of His great inventions, time itself. Not surprisingly, 'time nor tide' is a well-known expression which appears in Galway's favourite song, the older version of 'Galway Bay'. While time, as well as tide, awaits no man, the camera records a tiny instance of its passing each time the human hand entices its shutter to click. In the Galway context, the camera has been clicking now for over a century and a half.

No one knows exactly when a crude lens first filled itself with a western flavour, but tantalising clues offer some insight into the excitement engendered. One of the very first photographic images to appear in the Galway area shows a married couple facing the camera, operated perhaps by a landed gentry hand from the Blake estate near Oranmore just outside Galway city. It is not known exactly when John and Margaret Finn first faced that camera, but family tradition suggests the late 1840s or perhaps the early 1850s.

By the end of the nineteenth century, cameras were a prized possession of the upper classes, and time-wearied albums sometimes appear at auctions with photographs of such family groups, suitably attired, as they pose on mansion steps or family croquet courts. Although it would be many years before the common hand dared operate a camera shutter, commonalty was not entirely excluded from the magic of the glass plate.

The camera was a useful weapon against crime — offenders could be photographed and their true images placed on 'Hue and Cry' posters beside 'felons' wanted for political offences. Convicts too had their photographs affixed to official forms, the supreme symbol of Victorian efficiency. They are powerful images of a society wed solidly to the rock of conservatism, but weak in the realms of liberalism.

Important Galway city clergy also figured in these early photographs, such as Claddagh devotee Fr Tom Burke, named the 'Prince of Preachers' by Pope Pius IX because of his marvellous sermons, especially in America. Meanwhile, Fr

Peter Yorke from Long Walk, popular for his work in Irish trade union circles in that same 'land of the free', also appeared in an early photograph.

On the other hand, Queen's College Galway was eager to provide society with photographic studies of its leading academics when Catholics were still wary of its 'godless college' image and politicians questioned the university's viability in a fading western town. One of the most noteworthy depicted was John Elliot Cairnes, Professor of Jurisprudence and Political Economy, whose famous work, *The Slave Power*, was read the world over and influenced such strange bedfellows as Abraham Lincoln and Karl Marx!

Nor were students forgotten. Rather stilted photographs of them in their tall hats underlined an age when women found it difficult to gain access to the realms of higher education. One who broke this barrier, however, was Galwegian Alice Perry, who graduated from Queen's College Galway in 1906, the first of her sex to graduate in engineering in the UK. Her photograph highlights the changing times the new century would introduce — the female hand was lifting the latch of the open door now, and tea in the drawing-room of the Persses of Glenarde House on Taylor's Hill would never be the same again.

There was a stirring too amid the vanities of the lower classes. Having your 'picture' taken and displaying it on the Victorian mantlepiece was certainly in keeping with those 'upstairs'. Demand, of course, led to supply and towards the end of the nineteenth century, the Hill photographic studio in Henry Street was much frequented. Whether seated or standing stoically by the folded drapes of curtained backdrops, Galwegians faced the hooded camera and froze with time itself.

As the new century dawned, further photographic studios opened, including R.W. Simmons on William Street. Today sepia pictures from that studio gradually fade with time. Youthful faces of an Irish Volunteer or Corrib rower stare at us from the era of the horse and cart, when trams ran through streets filled with goods displayed openly in front of shops — the time of the 'lifter' was not yet nigh.

Not everyone could afford such photographic luxuries as a self-portrait, however, when a shilling was a good day's wage and pennies came from sweat instead of heaven. Yet image treasures of another type came to fill the mantlepiece with the mass-produced pictures we know today as picture postcards. A new industry was being born before the nation's eyes as the camera became a midwife to the craze for exact imagery of body and place, ironically at a time when Fine Art was dissolving elsewhere into Turner mists and Picasso cubes.

The famous Lawrence publishers led the way with some of the earliest Irish postcards, while the English company of Valentines published many well-known examples from their works in Dublin. On the home sod in Galway, local postcard-makers included McCullaghs, O'Gormans, Hares and, indeed, the *Connacht Tribune*, right up to the 1960s and Yann himself.

In all, it is estimated that over 3,000 different postcards of Galway city scenes have been created with many more smaller producers such as the 'Bon Bon', Salthill, bringing out their own series of pure nostalgia. While the early delights of Salthill itself and all its seaside charms were favourite studies, the famous Claddagh fishing village heard the camera click most often from professional and amateur photographers alike. When colour technology arrived from France in 1913, the swish of red petticoats amid the white and brown of thatch ensured that Claddagh charm would figure prominently in some of the earliest bi-chrome prints ever taken in Ireland.

Meanwhile, the ancient Church of St Nicholas and Lynch's Castle filled many an early lens, while in street scenes the paucity of traffic is a wonder to modern eyes. Tram lines, too, fill these initial commercial shots, often leading from the bustle of fair and market, themselves favourite subjects for the early photographer. There is more excitement also as the 'Cheap Jack' comes to make his market pitch from his cart of faded dreams. Here, at last, in 1893, we see the work of one of the first amateur photographers to 'snap' Galway as it was, for in the Maeve Frost Collection, now housed in Galway County Library, the mansion steps are being vacated and simple workers of the soil fill the camera lens.

This, then, is the power of the photograph because the hopes and aspirations of succeeding generations are etched in its myriads of dots, each snap capturing some special local moment in the passing of time, such as the coming of a British king or American president. Some of these same moments are important to the nation also, as the camera catches that historic occasion when Irish troops take over Renmore Barracks in the aftermath of the Fight for Independence.

Perhaps the camera is at its best when it records for posterity the youthful faces of those freedom fighters such as 'Baby' Duggan — men little more than boys who fought for love of country and died young for the cause.

Later, as World War II threatened these very shores, young men donned the uniform yet again — their faces just as determined to *seas an fód* (hold their ground) against an enemy from whatever source. Yet that same war left its mark on the city landscape as we note empty shipping berths and deserted streets, when people emigrated or simply died away. An air of despair hangs over the medieval heart of this former medieval city state, as once proud buildings fall into ruin and simple homes to damp decay. The camera captures it all, of course, its lens happy to record the bad as well as the best of times as long as the light is right.

History works in cycles, however, and as recessionary times fade away the camera catches that change in Galway's recent history as new factories, schools, shops and colleges open and give fresh hope for the future. Meanwhile up in Ballybrit, prize money and attendances grow ever larger, while St Patrick's Day parades take hours to pass and cultural festivals simply multiply.

Yes, the good times also figure prominently among these photographs, for happy faces at school functions or delighting in that sporting victory or annual dinner dance are part and parcel of simply 'us'. Religion also plays its part in our pictorial parade, whether it be the opening of Europe's last great stone cathedral, or women, freed from ever-ending housework, stepping it out in the old-style Corpus Christi procession.

The camera never lies, they say, so the following pictures, which conclude in 1979, recall a Galway that actually *was* and not simply imagined. See it as it was then, when people were poor in pocket but rich in heart.

1850s

The Finns of Maree

John (1787–1872) and Bridget, née Athy (1803–93) Finn of Maree, just outside Galway city, pose for one of the earliest photographs taken in the Galway district. John's mother was governess to the Blakes at Ardfry Castle, one of whom may have taken this photograph probably in the 1850s. John Finn is said to have built Tawin Bridge. (Courtesy Terry and Margaret Casey)

1860s

Robert O'Hara Burke

Pictured here is Robert O'Hara Burke, who was born in 1822, probably in Dominick Street, and whose father, James H. Burke, was mayor of Galway at the time. Robert led the first expedition to cross Australia, south to north, in 1860, but met a tragic end in 1861 at Cooper's Creek on the return journey. He is a major figure in Australia's history. (Courtesy William Henry)

1870s

John Elliot Cairnes

Although he died at the early age of fifty-one in 1875, John Elliot Cairnes, Professor of
Jurisprudence and Political Economy at Queen's College Galway from 1859–70, was
considered to be the leading economist in the world at the time of his death. His book, *The
Slave Power*, published in 1862, a powerful study of slavery in the 'Deep South', drew a letter
of appreciation from no less a person than Abraham Lincoln, President of the United States,
and more than a passing interest from Karl Marx. (Courtesy NUI, Galway)

Fr Tom Burke

Galway's most famous cleric, Fr Tom Burke
OP (1830–83), is pictured here wearing St
Dominick's 'white wool'. He founded a
noviciate and house of studies in Tallaght, Co.
Dublin, before spending eighteen months on
a lecture tour expounding the Catholic faith
and rebuking justification of England's
occupation of Ireland and her administration
of the affairs of that country. He was awarded
the title 'Prince of Preachers' by Pope Pius
IX. His statue stands today at the entrance to
the Claddagh. (Courtesy Tom Kenny)

University Students

Ivy is already evident on the walls of Queen's College Galway when this early photograph
of students was taken in 1872/3. The college first opened in 1849 with sixty-eight students
enrolled to study Chemistry, Natural History, Modern Languages, Celtic Studies,
Agriculture, English Law, Political Economy, Medicine, Surgery and Civil Engineering. Of
interest is the fact that the chair of Agriculture operated a co-operative type farm at Ardfry
near Oranmore. Most students of the time, however, studied Medicine. (Courtesy NUI,
Galway)

1880s

William King

William King, Professor of Mineralogy and Geology in Queen's College Galway from 1849–83, coined the term 'Neanderthal man' to describe what he judged to be a new hominid species after studying a fossil of a skull discovered in a cave in Bohemia. His conclusions, despite opinion to the contrary at the time, were proven to be correct a half a century after he died, and he drew glowing praise from L.S.B. Leakey in 1969 for his pioneering work. (Courtesy NUI, Galway)

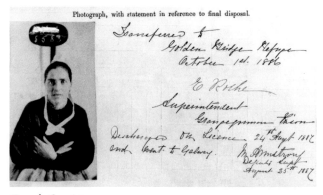

Photograph, with statement in reference to final disposal.

Female Convict

Convict No. 8583 stares out at us from prison where this photograph was taken in or just prior to 1886. This unfortunate woman is just one of many depicted by Geraldine Curtin in her book, *The Women of Galway Jail,* which tells the sad story of female criminality in 19th-century Ireland, with special reference to those incarcerated in Galway Jail between 1881 and 1891. (Courtesy Geraldine Curtin)

Claddagh Village

This unique photograph of 1888 shows water flowing through the later 'Big Grass' area of the old Claddagh fishing village. The section in front of the village towards the sea was filled in and became the open green area where geese used to gather, lines and nets were stretched and children played. (Courtesy National Museum)

1890s

Cheap Jack at the Fair
Great excitement is in the air as a Cheap Jack is photographed in 1893 at a fair in Galway city in one of a set of photographs presented by Mrs Maeve Frost to Galway County Library. People scramble all around the vendor's cart to get a view of what was on offer — a scene familiar the world over. (Courtesy Maeve Frost and Galway County Library)

Eglinton Street at the end of the 19th Century
Another Frost Collection photograph depicts Eglinton Street in 1893. People could stand on the roadway for a chat as the shawled lady with basket and tall-hatted man demonstrate here. Across the road, two policemen also have time for a few words outside the new police barracks, while in the distance a cart laden with seaweed is making its way along the cobbled channel with the 'Abbey' in the background. (Courtesy Maeve Frost and Galway County Library)

Washer Woman
This Frost Collection photograph shows a washer woman making her way in 1893 down past the Eglinton Canal bridge at St Joseph's Church. She holds a beatle in her hand, a wooden paddle for 'battering' wet clothing to remove dirt. She also holds her laundry bundle on her left arm, which she will wash at the washing station at the Spout Mór. The Spout Mór consisted of steps (recently uncovered) leading down directly to the water's edge at Pumpeen Lane. (Courtesy Maeve Frost and Galway County Library)

Potato Market

Once the humble 'spud' came into prominence in Ireland, especially at the start of the 19th century, its market potential was enormous. Here in this 1893 Frost Collection photograph, the weighing scales at the Small Crane off Williamsgate West is in full use weighing sacks of potatoes brought into the market from Barna and the surrounding countryside. (Courtesy Maeve Frost and Galway County Library)

Pig and Calf Market

Without the supermarkets of today, late 19th-century Galway had to rely on various types of outdoor markets as shown in this photograph of 1893. The pig and calf market in Eyre Square, while not as large as the cattle, sheep or turf versions, still engendered excitement as buyers, such as the gentleman in the top hat in this Frost Collection photograph, came looking for bargains. (Courtesy Maeve Frost and Galway County Library)

Woollen Socks Market

This wonderful Frost Collection photograph shows the female side of the typical 19th-century entrepreneurial 'twosome'. Thick, woollen stockings, in recent times a favourite with 'Sonny' Molloy's of High Street, are on sale on the open footwalk in Eglinton Street below where the Post Office is today. While her male counterpart was busy selling cattle, sheep or pigs elsewhere, the *bean an tí* sold 'the sweat of her brow' on what really was the open market! (Courtesy Maeve Frost and Galway County Library)

Flannel Market

Rough red flannel, a product once popular as an item of underwear in times gone by (its very coarseness caused the skin to redden and so warm up!), is recorded for posterity in this Frost Collection photograph of 1893. Taken where Eyre Street and Woodquay meet, potential buyers gather around a vendor whose simple stall has been set up outside the crumbling ruins of buildings depicted on the famous 1651 Pictorial Map of Galway. (Courtesy Maeve Frost and Galway County Library)

Turf Market

While there was also a turf market in Eyre Square, the one depicted here in this Frost Collection photograph of 1893 was in front of the Claddagh area known as the Garra Glas, where the fire station is today. Turf, with wood, was the only means of fire heating for the lower classes in 19th-century Galway — thus the importance of the turf market at the time. (Courtesy Maeve Frost and Galway County Library)

Fowl Market

Shawls are very much evident here at the fowl market in the last decade of the 19th-century in this Frost Collection photograph. Also to be seen are the old Claddagh-type cloak and the famous *práiscín* or rough apron so favoured by Claddagh women of the time. (Courtesy Maeve Frost and Galway County Library)

19th-Century Dress

This Frost photograph of 1893 shows the typical dress of the time as worn by Mr and Mrs Broderick from the Claregalway area. He is wearing a hard hat, shirt, waistcoat, breeches tucked inside his stockings and boots, while she sports the old-style cloak (with basket underneath) and the famous apron as they stroll along the tram track in Williamsgate Street after a *seisiún* at the fair in Eyre Square. (Courtesy Maeve Frost and Galway County Library)

Bridge Traffic

The Salmon Weir Bridge is practically empty of traffic except for this horse and cart slowly trundling across its rough surface in this Frost photograph of 1893. The passenger in the back holds the typical type of basket of the time, while behind her in the distance the Clifden Railway Line bridge across the Corrib is under construction. (Courtesy Maeve Frost and Galway County Library)

Prospect Hill

A very wide and mostly deserted Prospect Hill is depicted in this Frost photograph of 1893. While the houses on the right-hand side of the photograph appear the same today, all of the thatched houses on the left have disappeared. The cart on the left is beside the Hynes Pipe Factory and the three-storeyed building was once a police station. (Courtesy Maeve Frost and Galway County Library)

Visit of a Lord Lieutenant

The visit of a Lord Lieutenant was always an important occasion for town and gown. This was especially so to the 'budding' Queen's University Galway in the 19th-century, as this picture, taken in the 1890s, shows. Standing (*left to right*): Army officer, Prof. Alexander Anderson, — , Prof. Edward Townsend, Prof. Richard Kinkead, Prof. Philip Sandford, —, Prof. William Brereton, Prof. Isaac Lynham, Burser. Seated (*left to right*): Army officer, President T.W. Moffett, Lord Lieutenant Zeitland, Rev. James Fleetwood Berry and Prof. George Allman. (Courtesy NUI, Galway)

The 'Fomairí'

Once the harvest was in, farmers and their wives, both called the *fomairí*, came to Salthill in the autumn to 'take the airs and the waters'. The waters consisted of sea baths in buildings seen in the right background behind Patrick Callanan from Kilreekil. The famous 'Lazy Wall' where the women used to gather to chat is in the left background. Patrick wears the 'in' outfit of the times, i.e. a swallow-tail coat, breeches and Caroline hat. (Courtesy Galway County Library)

Dominican Convent Pupils

Young boarders in the Dominican Convent pose for this 1897 photograph. The girls with violins were taught by the Galway leader of the Royal Welsh Fusiliers' String Band. Back row (*left to right*): B. Geoghegan, M. Royston, N. Geoghegan, M. Reidy, M. Fogarty, M. Donnellan, C. Hughes. Middle row (*left to right*): K. Higgins, N. Mulligan, D. Rafferty, K. Mulligan, K. Culhan, N. McKenna, A. Staunton, L. Cronin, M. McKenna, D. Kilgariff, Delia Joyce, K. Tierney, M. Jones. Front row (*left to right*): M. Lydon, M. O'Dea, M. Smiddy, M. McAuliffe, B. Lydon, M. O'Connell, C. Geoghegan, P. Fagan, T. Geoghegan, A. O'Dea, T. O'Connell, E. O'Connell, J. Burke, A. Geoghegan. (Courtesy Sr Rose O'Neill OP and David Joyce)

1900s

Royal Visitors at Dillon's

The packed scene opposite Dillon's Corner in 1903 as King Edward V11 and Queen Alexandra are driven in open coach from the railway station to embark on the royal yacht in Galway Docks. An overhead banner proclaims: 'He loves the Green Isle and his love is recorded.' Dillon's family jewellery business, as well as decorating their premises with flags and bunting, proudly presented the Queen with a gold Claddagh ring in honour of the occasion.

Royal Visitors at the Docks
King Edward VII and Queen Alexandra leave Galway Docks by royal tender to be rowed
to the royal yacht anchored in Galway Bay. Local dignatories say farewell including, it
seems, Billie Binns, town engineer, pictured standing alone on the quayside. The royal
couple had earlier left the royal yacht in Killary Harbour and came to Galway on the
Galway/Clifden railway line.

Fr Peter Yorke
Born on Long Walk opposite the
Claddagh, Fr Peter Yorke (1864–1925)
became a fearless defender of the
oppressed, especially the Irish, in San
Francisco. He published a newspaper
expressing Irish and labour views there,
gaining the gratitude of Pope Pius X.
He is pictured here in 1901 with
nephews and nieces and other family
members in the Santa Cruz mountains.
(Courtesy Galway County Library)

Garra Glas

Summer time, as Claddagh inhabitants, including a child in the quaint pram, laze in the sun in front of the two-storey Raftery home in the Garra Glas area of the old Claddagh. The gleaming whitewash and thatch keep the little homes cool during the heat wave. (Courtesy National Museum)

Academic Chat

D'Arcy Wentworth Thompson, Professor of Greek at Queen's College Galway from 1864–1902, is pictured in his usual long coat and top hat on the Salthill Promenade. His conversation companion is thought to be Valentine Steinberger, Professor of Modern Languages at the university from 1886–1916. Although in Galway for over forty years, Steinberger was incarcerated during the initial years of World War I because of his German background. (Courtesy NUI, Galway)

College Hopes

Hatted students gather in front of Queen's University Galway as they contemplate what the new 20th century holds for them and their university. There were fewer than one hundred students attending as the new century dawned because Catholics were not encouraged to attend such 'godless colleges'. Public opinion had the university retained, however, and in 1908, the National University of Ireland and University College Galway (UCG) came into existence. The rest is history. (Courtesy NUI, Galway)

Alice Perry
While university attendance was mostly a male preserve in the 19th century, by 1906 Alice Perry, a native of Galway and one of three sisters attending the college, had the unique distinction of being the first female engineering graduate in the then United Kingdom. (Courtesy NUI, Galway)

1910s

Lynch's Castle

Time has taken its toll on this once proud building as Lynch's Castle appears dark and weary after centuries of occupation. Lynch mayors, who were said to have occupied this fine house, have long since gone. Kirwan's, the chandlers, had a shop on the ground floor when this photograph was taken, and Kilroe Mills on the Headford Road had debased the building further with a rather brash advertisement. (Copyright of the Royal Society of Antiquaries of Ireland)

Claddagh Navy Men
It was increasingly difficult for young Claddonians to make a living from fishing with the old style Claddagh hookers as the 20th century unfolded. Seeing jobs readily available in the British Navy, however, many joined up and saw service in World War I. Typical were these three O'Flaherty brothers from the Garra area of the Claddagh who are pictured here on leave in 1912. While Laurence (*left*) served on HMS *Victory* and was an expert gunner, John (*centre*) and Dominick served on HMS *Excellent*. (Courtesy Tony Flannery)

Irish Volunteer

Only a few years out of national school, Martin Crowe of Bohermore is pictured in 1919 in his Irish Volunteer uniform. Typical of the youth who took up arms at the time, Martin was arrested with fourteen others the week following the murder of Fr Michael Griffin in 1920, and was eventually sent to Ballykinlar detention camp in Co. Down. He was incarcerated there for over a year, before being released to participate in the Fight for Independence. He later emigrated to America where he became the travel announcer in Boston Railway Station.

The 'Mon' School Band

In this photograph of c.1910, Brother Brendan stands proudly beside his Monastery School band as the boys stand to attention in the school yard beneath the banner of the patron saint of Ireland. Matty Hynes of Eyre Street stands directly behind the bass drummer. (Courtesy Frank Hynes)

St Mary's College

The laying of the foundation stone of Galway's new diocesan seminary took place on 26 May 1910, and the solemn blessing of the building occurred on 25 August 1912. Its first president was Fr Peter Davis who, with a staff of seven, taught the initial intake of sixty-four boarding and seventeen day-pupils. Built mostly from Galway granite and thus in accord with its natural surroundings, the new college, designed by W.A. Scott, was an imposing edifice for its day. (Courtesy Galway Diocesan Archives)

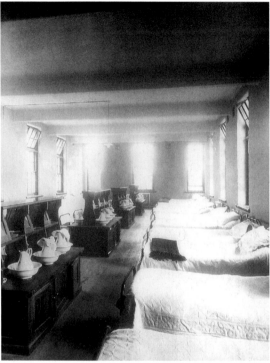

Cold Feet!

At least one student of St Mary's College had cold feet it seems, judging by the blanket left at the bottom of a bed in the upstairs dormitory. Plenty of daylight, fresh air and cold water in jug and bowl underline the rather spartan conditions, judged by modern standards, awaiting the new students who arrived in the college in 1912. (Courtesy Galway Diocesan Archives)

St Mary's Road

Only a stone wall and narrow roadway delineate where St Mary's Road is today in this photograph taken from the roof of the new St Mary's College in 1912. The white cottages of Raleigh Row can be seen in the distance (right), with the Jesuit Church and school evident in the background. On the left, Greally's College, formerly West House, can be seen standing alone in the background, while the nearby tall chimney of the Semple & Cloherty Sawmill and the tower of the Collegiate Church of St Nicholas stand proudly above the smoke rising from a thousand homes. (Courtesy Galway Diocesan Archives)

Aerial Photograph of University

Green fields still surround the original university building to the left, the famous Quadrangle, which first opened its doors to students in 1849. On the right, the new engineering block has just been completed in this photograph of the 1910s. The population of Galway city, then about 15,000, was the lowest since the coming of the Industrial Revolution to the city at the start of the 19th century. (Courtesy NUI, Galway)

1920s

City Corners

This familiar view presents inner city corners to the viewer, with the massive tower and spire of the Church of St Nicholas standing tall in the centre. On the right, the old Thimble Castle has a very wide opening on to Shop Street, while No. 1, on the left, has its doorway filled with merchandise — in this case, racks of shoes and boots. A once familiar sight in Galway, the 'corner boy' completes this nostalgic view of the past. (Copyright of the Royal Society of Antiquaries of Ireland)

Cpl Laurence Flaherty

Typical of the men who took part in the Fight for Independence and Civil War was Michael Flaherty of the old Claddagh fishing village. He joined the Free State troops and is pictured here in the early national uniform, complete with standard .303 rifle, bandoleer and leggings. He also sports a small crucifix hanging from the top right pocket of his uniform, 'just in case'! (Courtesy Tony Flannery)

Old IRA

The Fight for Independence is evidenced in this 1921 photograph of the 2nd Battalion of the First Galway Brigade IRA taken at Killeen Castle, just outside Galway city. This battalion consisted of Claregalway, Annaghdown 'A' and 'B' and Kilcoona companies, under Comdt Padhraic Feeney of Claregalway who is pictured here in uniform. Galway city personnel pictured include drill instructor W. Cunningham (*reclining right*), P. O'Brien of the County Buildings (*kneeling third right*), Michael Feeney, St Bridget's Place (*standing fourth right, centre row*) and John Melia, Woodquay (*second right, back row*).

Aerial View of Corrib Estuary

An Army Aer Corp photograph of 1928 shows Lough Atalia and the railway bridge in the foreground. Galway Docks is empty of shipping, but two Galway hookers can be seen heading out to sea. The old Claddagh fishing village is visible on the far shore, with the new ex-servicemen houses stretching away towards Grattan Road. A cycle track can be discerned in South Park, then known as the 'Swamp'. The iron barque *Lord Lyset* lies beached off Nimmo's Pier, soon to be rendered into scrap by the Hammond Lane foundry, while a German liner lies at anchor off Mutton Island.

Aerial View of Claddagh Village

Taken in 1928, when the old Claddagh fishing village was condemned under the various Health Acts, this picture shows the Big Grass area, with the Fairhill Road section leading off in the top left corner. The third main area, the Garra Glas, lies to the right of the three-storey Dominican Priory residence at the top right of the picture. Within twenty years these thatched houses would be replaced by the two-storey dwellings of the new Claddagh housing scheme, and a way of life was lost for ever.

Rowing Champion of Ireland

Pictured here is Tom Courtney of St Bridget's Terrace who brought the greatest rowing honours to Galway and the Commercial Boat Club, Woodquay, by winning the Eblana Cup, the equivalent of the Senior Sculls Championship of Ireland in 1920, 1921 and 1923. Only the Civil War prevented him from winning in 1922. He also won the Senior Sculls at Galway Regatta in 1914, 1919, 1920 and 1929. Sadly, the Commercial Boat Club ceased competitive rowing in the 1950s.

Fight for Independence

This unique photograph of active members of the IRA in the Galway area contains a rather puzzling caption which reads, 'Prisoners wounded in fight for dying comrade in Galway Jail with armed guard ...'. Five members display side arms. Included are Paddy O'Connor, Bohermore (*sitting, front left*) Tom Fleming, St Bridget's Tce (*middle row, left*) 'Baby' Duggan, Claregalway (*middle row, fourth left*) and Seán Turke, College Road (*extreme right*). (Courtesy Joe O'Connor)

Fr Tom Burke Hurlers

The Fr Tom Burke hurling team which won the City Challenge Cup in a sadly curtailed final in the Sportsground in 1929. Back row (*left to right*): Martin Mullaly, Peter Curran, Willie O'Donnell, Dominick Curran, James Carrick, James Moore. Third row (*left to right*): John Joe McNamara, John Costello, John Griffin, Tom O'Dea, Martin Griffin, John Moore, Martin Gannon, Paddy Curran, John O'Brien, Jim Sharkey, Tom Higgins, Michael John Noone. Second row (*left to right*): John Geary, Tom Griffin, Willie Curran (Capt.), Eddie Moore, Peter Griffin. Front row (*left to right*): Addlie Hynes, Geoff Murphy.

Claddagh Statue Procession

A historic day in the old Claddagh as Claddonians gather to watch girls in First Communion and Confirmation outfits walk in the procession leading to the installation of the ancient statue of 'Our Lady of Galway' in the Dominican Church in 1922. The statue can be seen today on the side altar to the left of the main altar in the Claddagh Church. (Courtesy Mary Julia Browne)

Lyon's Tower

This unique photograph shows the bastion that once defended the original circular Lyon's Tower in Eglinton Street. While the inner section facing the camera shows much deterioration, the outer walling is still intact and gives an idea of how impressive the original medieval city wall was. (Copyright of the Royal Society of Antiquaries of Ireland)

Claddagh Shyness

The Claddagh people in the past were always noted for their shyness, none more so than the children. The two photographed here reflect that shyness as they gaze in wonder at the camera and visitor. The thatched houses in the background have been newly whitewashed, and their position to one another shows the 'higgledy-piggledy' style of placement so beloved by artist and photographer alike. A shower of rain has just fallen. (Copyright of the Royal Society of Antiquaries of Ireland)

University Camogie

By the end of the 1920s, when this photograph was taken, camogie had taken its rightful place among University College sports. Pictured here are the UCG Camogie Ashbourne Cup intervarsity winners for 1928. Front row (*left to right*): Madge Tonry, Emma Gilligan, Maura Cooke. Middle row (*left to right*): Sheila Kennedy, Mary O'Brien, Violet Bodkin (Capt.), Molly Keegan, Bridget Crowe. Back row (*left to right*): Marguerite McCoy, Evelyn Walsh, Frances Geoghegan, Frances Burke and Mr Molloy, coach. (Courtesy NUI, Galway)

Military Barracks Takeover (1)

The culmination of the War of Independence in Galway came with the official takeover of Renmore Army Barracks by units of the Irish Free State Army after the British vacated the facility in 1922. The vanguard of the Irish troops is pictured here entering through the main gate behind a local boys' band, while comrades form a guard of honour. (Copyright *Connacht Tribune*)

Military Barracks Takeover (2)

The new Irish troops, still without uniforms except for the officers, stand to attention in the main parade ground, while the tricolour proudly flies above the turret in the background. Dismantled British army vehicles lie scattered in the foreground, indicating the sudden change in military affairs. (Copyright *Connacht Tribune*)

Memory of Fr Griffin
The tricolour flies above the doorway of No. 2 Mountpellier Terrace, Sea Road, in this historically important photograph of 4 December 1921, taken the day before the Treaty was signed in London. From here, just a year before, the popular curate Fr Michael Griffin was lured to his death by Crown Forces. Those in the centre (*front to back and left to right*) include: Seán Turke (in uniform), Fr Tom Burke, Éamon De Valera, Fr Bob O'Reilly, Harry Boland, Cathal Brugha, Dr Ada English, Larry Lardner, Fr Jimmy O'Dea, Eamonn Corbett, Miss Cashel, Capt. Padraic Kelly, Padraic Fahy, Tommy O'Grady, Paddy Arkins, Maggie Burke and Helena Concannon. (Courtesy Farrell's PhotoStudio)

'Baby' Duggan

Thomas Duggan, known as 'Baby' due to his youthful expression, was the first Commanding Officer of Renmore Barracks when it was vacated by the British Army after the Truce in 1922. Born in Roscam in 1899, he was active in the 1916 Galway Rising. On his release from Frongoch, he became First Brigade Quartermaster of the Old IRA in Galway. When the split came, he joined the republican side, set fire to Renmore Barracks and went on the run again. Captured, he went on hunger strike which greatly impaired his health. He died a young man in 1925. (Courtesy Seán Stewart)

New Versus Old

Ridges filled with potatoes run right up to the de-roofed little Claddagh home which awaits final demolition at the end of the 1920s. Already the nearby ex-servicemen houses are occupied, virtual mansions compared to the little thatched houses which sustained the old Claddagh fishing village for so long. Within a little over a decade or two all of these homes would disappear and a very important part of the built heritage of Galway would become a memory. (Courtesy Seán Stewart)

Postal Workers All

Indoor and outdoor staff are depicted in this photograph standing outside the former General Post Office in Eglinton Street. While managers and clerks are dressed in the normal suits of the 1920s, the postman on the left sports the early 'uniform' of cap, badge and bag, and holds his first round of letters in his hand. (Courtesy James Casserly)

Ex-servicemen Houses

Excitement grew in the Claddagh during the 1920s as returning ex-servicemen and sailors, many of whom had given excellent service to the British Army and Navy during World War I, were provided with new semi-detached houses, which dwarfed those of the old fishing village. Our picture shows construction work being carried out using wooden scaffolding and concrete blocks at Beattystown on Fairhill Road, one of the first large contracts for James Stewart Builders. (Courtesy Seán Stewart)

Pádraic Ó Conaire

Galway city's most famous writer in Irish, Pádraic Ó Conaire was born in 1882 and died in Dublin in 1928. In his short life of only forty-six years, Pádraic wrote many books, short stories, articles, and a column in the *Connacht Sentinel*. His famous limestone statue by Albert Power has enthralled visitors to Eyre Square since it was unveiled by Éamon De Valera in 1934. His best-loved work, *M'Asal Beag Dubh*, has been read by generations of Irish schoolchildren. (Courtesy Jack Cunningham)

1930s

Claddagh Furniture
'A dresser filled with shining delph' was a major status symbol in the old Claddagh fishing village. Here Nan Ryan is pictured with a fine example of delphware, which was often collected from the four corners of the earth by sons of the Claddagh who served in the British Navy about the time of World War I.

Claddagh Conversation

A quiet chat among the cobblestones, geese and hens in the Old Claddagh. The broom is laid aside as Sally O'Brien and Kate Ryan enjoy a chat over the half-door.

Claddagh Visitor

Nathalie Fournier, mother of Etienne Rynne, former Professor of Archaeology, NUI, Galway, is pictured here in 1932 sitting on a 'colya' or bollard in front of the Dominican Church. Two men chat at the corner pillar of the church grounds, while youngsters play hurling in the small green area bounded on the left by the tin-roofed bakery of the Murphy family, the homes of the Mullaly, Cloherty and King families, and the gables of the homes of the Carrick, Morgan and Moore families. (Courtesy Prof. Etienne Rynne)

Máirtín Mór McDonogh

Máirtín Mór McDonogh was the leading merchant and manufacturer in Galway during the early part of the 20th century. Elected a Cumann na nGael TD in 1927 and 1933, he was an ardent opponent of trade unionism. Nevertheless, at his death in 1934 hundreds of his workers walked in his funeral cortège to Forthill Cemetery. It was the largest funeral seen in Galway since the death of Fr Peter Daly in 1868. Among his many achievements he ensured that the Galway Races survived the demise of the landed gentry to become the success they are today. (Courtesy Thomas McDonogh & Sons)

Grealishtown

It is easy to see why the cluster of houses opposite the New Cemetery was known as Grealishtown from this photograph taken at the start of the 1930s. Built by a man named Grealish, the houses stand separated from the rest of Bohermore on the left by a high country wall, and on the right by the shells of half completed houses. Meanwhile, Mrs Mary Meaney, Renmore, stands proudly beside her brother Liam, who subsequently emigrated to Canada. (Courtesy Mary Meaney)

Setting Sail

One of the delightful *gleoiteogí* from the Old Claddagh is silhouetted on a sparkling sea as she heads out into Galway Bay. Beyond her, a larger Claddagh hooker, now more generally known as a Galway hooker, is already under full sail for the fishing grounds.

Sail Trawlers

The tranquil surface of Galway Docks in the late 1930s is disturbed in this photograph as two sail/steam trawlers enter the Commercial Dock. The one on the right is the *Lord Marmion*, which was owned by Joe O'Donnell, New Docks. The wake behind her suggests she is side-towing the other vessel whose engine may have broken down. (Courtesy Peter Cloherty)

The Age of the Bicycle

O'Brien's Bridge looks rather deserted in this photograph taken in the early 1930s. The traffic consists simply of two cyclists going in the opposite direction. Willie Crowe is shown coming towards us on his version of a 'High Nellie', complete with bell, as he makes his way down to his home in Woodquay. The bridge seems very wide, while in the distance, the pub contains the Galway Arms memorial between its upstairs' windows, a plaque which once was displayed on a gate tower over the medieval 'Great West Bridge' on this site. (Courtesy Maggie Crowe)

McDonogh Group

A happy staff photograph of Thomas McDonogh & Sons personnel taken on the steps of the Great Southern Hotel in the late 1930s. Perhaps they are is going on a day's outing by rail and are bringing their own musicians with them. Joseph Cloonan from St Bridget's Terrace is pictured on the extreme right. (Courtesy Mrs Kathleen Cloonan and James Casserly)

Commerce Class

Final year commerce class of 1939 takes time out for a photograph. Seated (*far left*) in one of the rooms in the old Quad is Christopher Townley, later college librarian from 1960 to 1982. Standing behind him is Prof. MacBryan, Dean of Commerce at the time. (Courtesy NUI, Galway)

Dogfish Lane

This photograph of Dogfish Lane first appeared in the *Connacht Sentinel* on 15 January 1935 with the caption, 'A picturesque corner of the Old Claddagh, which is fast disappearing with the progress of the new housing estate.' The main reason for the demise of the village is evident in the sanitation channel running down to the estuary. Condemned under the prevailing Health Acts in 1928 for not having internal sewerage facilities, the village and this quaint lane, which housed the Harte, Higgins, Cooke, O'Donnell, O'Connor, Rushe, Concannon and Moore families, would soon became a part of history. (Copyright *Connacht Tribune*)

'Mon' Hurling

The Monastary School hurling team which won the Dean Considine City Schools' Cup in 1935. Back row (*left to right*): Michael John Geraghty (Grealishtown), M. Browne (Prospect Hill), Paddy Hennigan (St Patrick's Avenue), H. Trill (St Patrick's Avenue), P. Casserly (Grealishtown), W. Molloy. Middle row (*left to right*): Peter Griffin (Claddagh), S. Minihan (Nun's Island), Michael 'Cairo' Kelly (Bohermore), Charlie Hughes (Prospect Hill), O. Trill (St Patrick's Avenue), Seán Duggan (College Road, later to achieve An Post/GAA Hall of Fame 2002 award and be depicted on an Irish stamp), Michael John Healy (Henry Street). Front row (*left to right*): Seán Fox (Bohermore) and Eamon Molloy (Woodquay). The manager was Brother Killeen. (Courtesy Seán Duggan)

The 'Unknown' Worker

While long hours were the norm for Galway workers during the 1930s, often for small wages, this group of workers in one of Thomas McDonogh's fertiliser stores takes time out for a rather rare photo call. While only one, Michael McGrath (*standing, second left*), can be identified, one will certainly never be, as his face is covered from behind with a workmate's cap as a prank. (Courtesy James Casserly)

Galway Blazers

This early 1930s photograph shows the County Galway Hunt (the Blazers) riding under the Galway/Clifden railway bridge at Forster Street. The bridge is lined with excited spectators, while in the background the original spire of St Patrick's Church is clearly visible. The former Magdalene Asylum building is to the right. (Courtesy Farrell's PhotoShop)

The Merryweather Fire Engine

A giant step forward in the history of fire fighting in Galway is captured in this photograph with the arrival of the Merryweather fire engine to the former fire station in Bowling Green. Frank Dolan is the driver, with Tim Duggan sitting beside him. Other members include: Joe Philbin, 'Towser' McLoughlin, M. Philbin, P. Hughes, N. Glynn, M. Cloherty and P. Philbin. It is the era before uniforms were issued. This quaint fire tender is now in an English museum. (Courtesy Frank Dolan)

Handing Over of Jail

Eamon Corbett, Chairman of Galway County Council, is pictured (*right*) handing over the keys of the former Galway county and city jails, which closed in 1939, to Bishop Michael Browne. Members of the clergy, including Canon Glynn next to the bishop, and council members look on. Just over a quarter of a century later, Galway Cathedral would rise majestically on the site. (Courtesy Diocesan Archives)

McNally Crew

Despite some mutilation, this photograph taken in September 1932 records one of the early work crews of McNally Contractors as they take a welcome break during the renovation of a bank building. Jack Stewart Ltd was another construction company at the time, which celebrated one hundred years in business in 2002. (Courtesy Jimmy Mannion)

All Dressed Up

Four young men relax by the railings of the Eglinton Canal above the lock gates at Parkavera. All are impeccably dressed in three-piece suits, while three sport fashionable soft hats and ties. The young men wait for their lady friends, whom they will row up to the River Corrib, perhaps to the annual regatta, in the moored boats behind them. The Semple & Cloherty sawmill can be seen in the background. (Courtesy Jimmy Mannion)

Chamber of Commerce

Despite recessionary times, the Chamber of Commerce met regularly during the 1930s to encourage and promote trade and industry in Galway city. Seated (*left to right*): P.P. Shee, M.J. Crowley, Philip O'Gorman, J.S. Young, J. O'Kelly-Lynch, T.J.W. Kenny (President), E.K. Jackson, J.S. Conroy, Martin (Máirtín Mór) McDonogh, S. Corbett, R.A. Tennant. Behind chairman, standing: W.S. Fitzgerald (secretary), seated: Thomas Woods and M. T. Donnellan. (Courtesy Galway Chamber of Commerce and Industry)

Rail Freight Workers

Ever since the first train rolled across the Lough Atalia Bridge in 1851, hundreds of Galwegians and others have found permanent employment 'working on the railway'. Included among those taking time off for this photograph after loading a freight wagon in the late 1930s are road freight 'pioneers' T. Higgins, Matt Darcy, H. McFadden, Pat Nee, M. Barrett, D. O'Halloran and P. Browne. (Courtesy Martin Quinn)

Champion Rowers

Pictured here are the Emmets Crew at their clubhouse, Woodquay, in 1931. Included in the crew, mostly from Menlo, are: (*front, left to right*) Seán Faherty, Seán Connell, Martin Tierney, Malachy Ward, Mike Lawless. Back row (*left to right*): Tom Browne, Tommy Savage, Mike Ward, Mike Faherty, J. 'Ginger' Connell. This rowing crew, the most successful in Galway's history, won the IARU Senior Eights in 1929 and 1931. (Courtesy James Casserly)

Eyre Square Rally

No, this is not a car rally at the top of Eyre Square or for that matter a gathering of the Mafia! The platform set up in front of the Bank of Ireland tells us that a political meeting is in progress as loud-speakers spread the gospel to the converted. This is just one of many such meetings which Eyre Square witnessed in the early part of the 20th century. (Courtesy Martin Quinn)

1940s

Mutton Island

Mutton Island Lighthouse which directs shipping into Galway Harbour. This picture was taken in 1946 by Bill Scanlan, son of the lightkeeper, Thomas Scanlan, who was stationed on the island from 1943 to 1951. The high wall protected the lighthouse and tower from the sea. To the left of the house stands the flag-pole, which was used to signal the harbour installation in times of difficulty. (Courtesy Bill Scanlan)

Servicing Mutton Island

Lightkeeper Thomas Scanlan and his wife, Isabella, greet Jim Fleming as he guides his *gleoiteog* filled with provisions from Galway to the island's narrow pier in this 1947 photograph. Martin Fleming stands in the bow of the boat, while passenger Phil Keane enjoys her day out on Galway Bay. (Courtesy Bill Scanlan)

Eoin 'of the Quays'

Last in the line of the old kings of the Claddagh, Eoin 'of the Quays' Concannon, who died in 1954, is pictured sitting on his favourite 'colya' or bollard, flanked on the left by Eddie Shea of Abbeygate Street and on the right by Willie Crowe of Woodquay. The masts of two Galway hookers as well as the hulks of early trawlers berthed at Long Walk in the background recall the rich maritime history of the Claddagh. (Courtesy Maggie Crowe)

Army/Garda Personnel

The early 1940s was a time of war when Ireland stood neutral amid the belligerent nations. To uphold its neutrality, its shores had to be defended. Pictured here is a cross-section of military and police in the Galway city area. Many, however, were willing to *seas an fód* (hold their ground) against all comers whether from German or from Allied Forces. Guard Walsh, who later became a famous Galway policeman, is pictured sitting third from the left at the front. (Courtesy Tom Walsh)

Spanish Arch

A rather decrepit-looking Spanish Arch greets the camera lens at the end of the 1940s. Stones have been loosened by age since this section of the city walls was erected in 1584, and weeds grow in profusion. A portion of the blocked-up 'Blind Arch' (*an Póirse Caoch*) can be seen on the right, while in the distance the old gas light standard, occupied homes and store were still in use. (Courtesy Monica Wallace)

Buttermilk Lane
Children (one with bare feet) gather to play in Buttermilk Lane, the location of Walter Macken's famous play, *Mungo's Mansion*. Pedestrians, cyclists and a pram also inhabit this famous Galway thoroughfare as the summer sun beams down and captures a priceless moment in time. (Courtesy Monica Wallace)

Claddagh Pump

Modernity in the shape of an iron water pump (instead of a well or streamlet) at the gable end of the Mannion home is already evident in this Garra Glas section of the Claddagh, the last area to be cleared of its ancient traditional buildings after this photograph was taken in 1941. The house in the centre belonged to the Cubbard family, while that on the left was home to the Flaherty family. The Dominican Church occupies the distant space. (Courtesy Monica Wallace)

Claddagh Peace

This photograph of July 1941 continues the quiet corner of the Garra Glas area of the Old Claddagh. The houses from the left include those belonging to the Mannion, Folan, Conneely and Nee families, while the home of the Collins family forms an angle with the rest. This area is now occupied by the Galway Fire Station, with the road to the right leading up Fairhill Road. (Courtesy Monica Wallace)

Galway Provisions

Aran Islanders berth beside the *Dún Aengus* steamship in the 1940s before unloading precious commodities. At that time the tender, only three hours out from Galway, had to anchor offshore because of a lack of pier facilities in Aran. Despite rough conditions at times, commodities as delicate as eggs were successfully transferred between currachs and the tender thanks to the seamanship of the islanders. (Courtesy Monica Wallace)

SS Moyalla

One of Galway's favourite visitors, the SS *Moyalla* makes her way into Galway Docks. She sports the word 'Eire' on her side together with the Irish flag to signify her neutrality during World War II. Having survived the conflict, she ran aground on the Margaretta Shoal off Blackrock, Salthill, in February 1946. Although many salvage operations of her cargo and fittings were subsequently carried out, portions of the wreck can still be seen at very low tide. Some people today call the shoal the 'Moyalla' rocks! (Courtesy Peter Cloherty)

End of the Moyalla

The funnel and superstructure of the SS *Moyalla* are pictured here just above the water line at low tide shortly after she grounded on the Margaretta Shoal. That the end of this once familiar visitor to Galway Docks has finally arrived is made clear by the rather startling graffiti already painted on her main funnel: 'Help, Free beer for all'! (Courtesy Peter Cloherty)

Fr Griffin's Football Winners

Just eight months after being formed in Galway city, the new Fr Griffin Gaelic Football Club went on to win the first of its seven county titles in 1948. Standing (*left to right*): Pa Scully, Tom Brady, Aidan Corrigan, 'Staff' Lally, Seán Kindillon, Redmond Newell, Mick Flaherty, Paddy Lawlor, Fr Tom Parker, Mick Fenton, Seamus Reidy, Mick Dowling, Mick Lynch, Gerry Reidy (Trainer), Willie Naughton. Kneeling (*left to right*): Martin Kilmartin, Paddy Higgins, Paddy O'Brien, Jimmy Ward (Capt.), Austin Roche, J.J. Walsh, Paddy Fitzmaurice, Seamus O'Rourke, John Davy, Mick Collins. (Courtesy Paddy O'Brien)

Bus Drivers

Public transport by bus first came to Galway city with the Irish Omnibus Company, later replaced by the ironically named Great Southern Railway Company, before Córas Iompar Éireann came into being in 1945. Here are pictured GSR bus personnel, resplendent in their new uniforms: (*left to right*) John McEvoy, Tom Duffy, Miko O'Flaherty, Walter Burke, Jack O'Callaghan, Val Flaherty and Dick O'Driscoll. (Courtesy James Casserly)

Deserted Docks

Gathering war clouds are already evident in this scene of the Galway Docks as the huge coal unloaders lie unused on the Commercial Dock quayside. The trawler, *Lord Marmion*, lies on her port side as badly leaking dock gates allowed the water to escape during low tide. An air of abandonment lies over the once bustling harbour, which saw very few ships call during World War II. (Courtesy Peter Cloherty)

Blessing of the Bay 1940s Style
The last remaining Galway hookers of the old Claddagh fishing fleet gather around a steam trawler carrying the Dominican priest who will carry out the traditional blessing for a good harvest from the sea. Taken in July 1940, this photograph shows one of the last great gatherings of the traditional boats as the arrival of trawlers and their modern way of fishing heralded the end of the old Claddagh fishery. (Courtesy John Monahan and Nora Fennell)

Neck and Neck
The war is over now and people can really enjoy the Galway Races of 1946, especially when local lad Mickey Tully won the Galway Hurdle clad in the Corinthians rugby jersey astride his own Fair Pearl on the right. Here he is pictured just about to get the better of The Jungle ridden by Danny Morgan, the 1945 winner. Sadly, Mickey lost the race on a technicality. (Courtesy Jack Mahon and Galway Races' Committee)

Oranmore Castle

Pictured here is Oranmore Castle on the outskirts of Galway city prior to its purchase in 1947 by writer Anita Leslie King, wife of Bill King, a submarine commander during World War II and also an author of note, who made a famous solo sailing trip around the world. Daughter Leonie King, a well-known artist, is married to Alec Finn of de Danann music fame, and both now live in the restored tower house. In 1574 the castle was a stronghold of the Clanricarde Burkes and was much involved in the Parliamentarian wars. Later the Athys and Blakes gained possession of the castle. (Courtesy Monica Wallace)

Galway Woollen Mills

Here we picture Martin McDonagh of Bohermore at work in the Galway (Flynn's) Woollen Mill at Newtownsmyth in the 1940s. The mill was started by Fr Peter Dooley PP of St Patrick's in 1883, and gave much-needed employment at the time. This mill and Lydon's Woollen Mill in Dominick Street were the last in a long line of mills which originally operated from water power. Martin is surrounded by looms and other machinery, all of which was destroyed by fire in the 1950s. The site is now occupied by the Mercy Convent Secondary School. (Courtesy Farrell's Studio)

Galway Rowing Club

Members of the Galway Rowing Club, Woodquay, pictured at an end of season get-together outside the clubhouse in the early 1940s. Three generations of 'Barrahalla' fellows proudly gather around the numerous trophies won by club members. The famous rowing coach, Jim 'Ruacán' Heaney, sits directly behind the third boy from the right, and behind him stands Jim Reddington, a former mayor of Galway. (Courtesy Jack Cunningham)

1950s

Claddagh Drinkers

A happy gathering of Claddagh 'fellas' in the former Philip Coyne's pub at Raven Terrace in a photo taken by Nell O'Toole in 1957. The occasion seems to be a rather formal one, as many suits and ties are evident. Standing (*left to right*): Ladneen Curran in overcoat (later to be elected king of the Claddagh), — , Eddie Moore, — , Bartley Healy, Mr Walsh, — , Peter Flaherty, Paddy O'Toole. Sitting to rear (*left to right*): ? Harte and Máirtín Golden. In front (*left to right*): John O'Brien, Johnny Walsh and Michael Scofield. (Courtesy Thomas Holohan and Michael Mackey)

Truelight *and Blessing of Bay*

Martin Oliver sails out in 1958 from the Claddagh with a full complement of priests and local folk for the Annual Blessing of the Bay in his famous Galway hooker, *Truelight*. Pictured are Fr Moran and Fr Leahy, Dominicans, while Willie Folan (holding hat) and a host of youngsters look forward to the ceremony. The *Truelight* was sold the following year and the last hooker to be built for the Claddagh by Sean Rainey, a sturdy boat which survived the 1927 Cleggan disaster gale, sailed away into history. (Courtesy Peter Riddell)

Commercial Boat Club Group

Group photograph of members of the Commercial Boat Club, Woodquay, taken in the early 1950s. The club was founded in 1875 mainly as a rowing club, but the photograph shows trophies won by members for lawn tennis and billiards as well. Pat Horan, the president, is seated at the table (*centre*), while Seán Turke, an old IRA veteran, is seated on the left.

Angling Preparation

All set for a day's angling on Lough Corrib are Jimmy Maloney, John E. Colleran and Kruger Maloney. They are pictured getting ready on the shore at the Commercial Boat Club, Woodquay. While the traditional long trolling rod is evident, Jimmy Maloney in wellingtons is pictured setting up one of the new-fangled fixed spool reels and short fibre-glass spinning rods, which, in time, superceded the old wooden trolling reels and cane rods. Behind them open water extends all the way to the Dyke Road, and beyond lies open countryside where the Galway Shopping Centre is today. (Courtesy Kevin O'Toole)

The Weigh-in

Excitement fills the air as interested onlookers view the weigh-in at the Annual Bráithreacht na Coiribe Mixed Grill Competition held on the last Sunday of April 1958. Presenting their catch in the photograph are Neill Boyle (Jnr) and Pádraic Ó Máille in his famous Aran tweeds. Among the spectators are Peter Cooke, Paddy O'Toole, Miceál Thornton, Pat Lynskey and a very young Pádraic McGrath. (Courtesy *Connacht Tribune*)

'Niko' Dolan and Dray

All spruced up is CIE employee 'Nicko' Dolan, his faithful horse Kilraine and Guinness dray filled with thirty-three barrels of porter as they prepare to leave the Guinness depot off Lough Atalia Road to participate in the famous An Tóstal festival, a popular tourist attraction during the 1950s. (Courtesy Christy Hession)

Claddagh Film Extras

These four Claddagh ladies (*from the left*) Máim Golden, Mary Fallon, Margaret Jordan/Conneely and Agnes McDermot, were employed as extras in the film, *The Rising of the Moon*, which was shot in the 1950s. Two wear the black mourning shawl of the Claddagh, while the others display the wide variety of the Sunday shawl once so common in the old fishing village. (Courtesy Tony Flannery)

Michael John Burke

One of the great characters of Galway in the middle of the 20th century was Michael John Burke from Shantalla. The hat and coat worn by Michael John emphasise his navy background. He is pictured here with Mr Curran of Henry Street (*left*) and John Crowe, Bohermore (*right*), at Galway Docks as the yacht *Aisling* left for Vancouver on 1 May 1952. Noted for his sartorial elegance at all times, Michael was also famous for the many outlandish stories of his past life.

Soccer Stalwarts

Hibernians soccer team, winners of the Connacht Cup in 1952, are pictured in Terryland Park on that special day in the club's history. Back row (*left to right*): Brod Trill, Mike Fox, Jackie McSweeney, Jimmy Glynn, Paddy Kelly, Martin McDonagh, James McDonagh, Charlie O'Halloran, Mick Stiffe. Front row (*left to right*): Peter Holmes, Mike Messenger, Mickie O'Connor, Peter Laffey, John Browne, Stephen Mannion, Pete Powell, Gail Holmes, Joe Cunningham. Mascot ? Devereaux.

Joe Flynn, Barber

The hair cream jars in the window and the binary coloured pole over the door tell, just as much as the name, that this premises is one of the hairdressing salons operating in Galway during the 1950s. The proprietor Joe Flynn, on the right, stands with a friend outside his premises on Prospect Hill. Joe did a roaring trade with farmers during fair days which were held in nearby Eyre Square and spread right up to his premises. (Courtesy James Casserly)

CIE Retirement

Group taken at Galway Railway Station on 28 July 1959 on the occasion of the retirement of Martin McGrath, the first CIE bus driver to retire in Galway. Back row (*left to right*): — , F. Walshe, J. Garvey, P. Griffin, P. O'Brien, P. Furey, C. Donoghue, W. Spelman, T. Callinan, J. Fullard, M. McGrath. N. Lally, J. O'Connor, C. Rodgers, J. Dowd, W. Lyne, M. McAvaddy, P.J. Carroll, D. Timothy, M. O'Connor, A. Holland, W. Mahon. Front row (*left to right*): P. Brazil, P. Geoghegan, J. Monaghan, J. Sweeney, J. Callaghan, G. Burke, H. D'Arcy and B. Keaveney. (Courtesy James Casserly and Copyright *Connacht Tribune*)

Church of St Nicholas

A rare sight of the Church of St Nicholas is presented in this 1950s view with no Shambles Barracks (removed earlier in the century) or St Patrick's National School (built in 1954) to block the view in the middle background of a photograph taken on O'Brien's Bridge. Bicycles were still in the ascendancy when this Yann postcard photograph was taken on a fine summer's day. (Courtesy Owen Quinn)

Eyre Street Family

A happy Hynes family with friends stand in an empty Eyre Street. Back (*left to right*): Martin Hynes (last proprietor of the Racquets Court in Middle Street), Mary Hynes, Martin's wife Annie, relation Eileen Kinneavy and Dick O'Flaherty. Front: Eileen and Sean Hynes. Although the stone facade of Tommy Hanley's pub still stands, Roches Stores now occupies all the remaining buildings which belonged then (*from the left*) to Mrs Forde, the Concannon family, Warde's Garage in the gap, Mary Hynes, Nora O'Boyle, Mrs Lane and Poniard's Ivy Hotel at the end. (Courtesy Frank Hynes)

Town and Country Meet

Ancillary events during the Galway Horse Show in the Sportsground in 1957 include stock judging at the College Road wall end, with appropriate thatched houses in the background. Included are Pat Crowe, Tom Fahy, Tom Burke, Peter Griffin (with dairy shorthorn), Michael Dunne, Tom Clancy, Pat Kennelly, Martin Divilly, Frank Cosgrave (with cow), Paddy Fahy (with cow), Peter Codyre, Luke Small, Patrick Broderick and Danno Fahy. (Courtesy Niamh Ó Dochartaigh)

Browne to Brown!
Here we see the Galway All-Ireland Championship Cup being presented to Ian Dudgeon with Mr Brown by Bishop Michael Browne of Galway at the 1957 Horse Show in the Sportsground, College Road. Present also (*from left*) are Ned Carroll (hon. sec.), J.D. Whelan, with Patrick Daly (judge on dray), Ralph Langan with daughter, Martin Divilly and Mr Hynes from Oranmore. (Courtesy Niamh Ó Dochartaigh)

Air Tragedy
This sad photograph shows the mass burial of victims of a Dutch airliner which crashed off the west coast on 19 August 1958. Interments took place in the New Cemetery at Bohermore. Here Irish army troops are pictured carrying the coffins into the mass grave in the Protestant section of the cemetery, while thousands of onlookers pay their last respects. In the background the tall chimney of the hat factory can be seen. (Copyright *Connacht Tribune*)

Leisurely Eyre Square

Time certainly was not of the essence when this photograph was taken in the late 1950s. Pictured here is a section of the upper garden of the old Eyre Square, then enclosed by railings. Away from traffic, this area was an oasis of tranquillity where one could sit in peace and read the paper or rest the pram among the fragrance of flowers. (Copyright *Connacht Tribune*)

Jail Handover

An important moment in the ecclesiastical history of Galway was the handing over of the key of the former County Jail by Bishop Michael Browne to developer John Sisk in 1958, so that the building of Galway Cathedral could commence on the site. On the left is Fr Spellman, while to the right stands foreman Mr J. Lillis and Canon Glynn. (Copyright *Connacht Tribune*)

Salthill Currach Racing (1)
An Tóstal, the National Irish Cultural Festival of the 1950s, introduced the sport of the islands — currach racing — to the city, when special races involving the frail craft were held at Salthill. Thousands thronged the shoreline to see the traditional craft in action as here at Blackrock. In the background the former Golf Links Hotel can be seen, with Blackrock House in the distance. (Copyright *Connacht Tribune*)

Salthill Currach Racing (2)
The races are over and prizes are presented to the various winners by Mr J.A. Costello in front of the Golf Links Hotel. Also present is the Mayor, Peter Greene, while among the spectators are Seán McSweeney, later principal of Fr Griffin Road Technical School, and Michael Hannon of Woodquay, a staunch follower of outrigger rowing. (Copyright *Connacht Tribune*)

Galway Plate Winner

Winner and presenter are reflected in the gleaming silver of the Galway Plate as Mr J.S. Young, chairman of the Race Committee, presents the famous trophy to Mrs B. Biddle after her horse, Knight Errant, ridden by Bobby Beasley, won the Galway Plate at the 1957 meeting. The same combination went on to win the 1958 Galway Hurdle. Also in the picture are Alderman M. O'Flaherty and Mr J.D. Naughton, members of the committee. (Courtesy Jack Mahon and Galway Races' Committee)

Claddagh End

The end is really in sight now for the last remaining section of the Garra Glas area of the Claddagh fishing village in this 1950s photograph. The Flaherty home, pictured earlier in the 1940s section, has made way for Pakie Sullivan's garage where he kept his truck. The Sullivan home is to the left of the garage. All would come crumbling down by 1956 to make way for Galway's new fire station, which now occupies the site. (Courtesy Farrell's PhotoStudio)

Shop Street Fire

Galway Fire Brigade members bravely tackle the huge fire which destroyed the Brennan and Commins retail premises on Shop Street in 1952. While flames gush dramatically out of a side door, both premises are already gutted and only the medieval stone plaque between the upstairs windows of Commins's building has survived the flames. This fire was a harbinger of the much larger conflagration which almost destroyed the city centre in 1971. (Courtesy Frank Dolan and copyright *Connacht Tribune*)

New Fire Service Facilities

Fire Service personnel proudly pose before a new fire tender as well as the new fire station which replaced a major portion of the Garra Glas area of the old Claddagh fishing village by the middle of the 1950s. Back row (*left to right*): Joe Dolan, Michael Tierney, Michael Tuohy, Alex McDonald, Niko Dolan, Paddy Furey, 'Chick' Gillan and Martin Crehan. Front row (*left to right*): Michael Browne, Jim Dolan, Seán Cleary, Brendan Sugrue (Chief Fire Officer), Jack Lillis, Paddy Naughton and George Dolan. (Courtesy Frank Dolan)

Rosary Priest

Fr Patrick Peyton was born in the parish of Attymass, Co. Mayo, on 9 January 1909 and was ordained a priest in Notre Dame in America in 1941. Soon after, he launched a crusade to promote the family rosary, using radio networks and speaking at huge rallies all over the world. Here, on 9 May 1954, he is pictured speaking to thousands of followers, fronted by members of the Children of Mary, who had gathered at Ballybrit Race Course to hear his special message. (Courtesy Galway Diocesan Archives)

Chamber of Commerce and Industry

By the 1950s the importance of attracting industry to Galway was a main item on the agenda for each Chamber of Commerce and Industry meeting. The number of industrial estates in Galway today are testimony to the pioneering work of the following (*from left*): P. J. O'Donoghue, J. Owens, J. Fahy, J. Cheevers, M. O'Higgins, G.D. Naughton, G. Maume, G.I. Corbett (president), J. Allen, M. O'Flaherty, P.M. O'Beirn, J. Brennan, P. Ryan, J. Burke and J. Lydon. Standing: G.H. Warner (secretary). (Courtesy Galway Chamber of Commerce and Industry)

Patrician Musical Society (PMS)

A Patrician Musical Society rehearsal of the men's chorus for the *Pirates of Penzance* is in full swing in 1957 under the baton of 'Sonny' Molloy in this photograph, which features Suzanne 'Do Do' Courtney on the piano, with lead singer Gerry Glynn beside her looking down at the piano keys. The society, which commenced in 1952, has entertained Galway audiences for fifty years now with annual performances, mostly in the old and new Town Halls. (Copyright *Connacht Tribune*)

Industrial Hope

After nearly a hundred years in the industrial wilderness following the collapse of its water-powered industrial base, fresh hope came to the workforce of Galway city in the form of a new textile factory, which opened at Sandy Road in 1958. Known as the cotton factory, it heralded the industrial success of Galway today. Pictured here facing left are John Gorman, Bohermore, and Des Shaughnessy, Eyre Street, as they work in the screen printing section of the huge factory. (Copyright *Connacht Tribune*)

Taibhdhearc na Gaillimhe

Galway's unique theatre, Taibhdhearch na Gaillimhe in Middle Street, opened its doors to the public on 27 August 1928 with the staging of Mícheál Mac Liammóir's play, *Diarmuid agus Gráinne*. Since then many famous personalities have trodden its boards, including Siobhán McKenna in *Joan of Arc*, staged in 1952. She is pictured here to the right, on the famous stage, armed with a sword forged by Fintan Coogan, the well-known politician and blacksmith from New Road. (Copyright *Connacht Tribune*)

The Rising of the Moon

Black and Tans and police gather at the doorway of a house on Long Walk beside the Spanish Arch in a raid reminiscent of those that occurred in Galway during the Troubles. However, it is the 1950s now and the people in this photograph are actors taking part in the film, *The Rising of the Moon*, one of the many films shot on location in Galway during the twentieth century. (Courtesy Ethna Griffin)

Central Hospital

Pictured here is the front facade of the main block of the Central Hospital in 1956 prior to its demolition. The Central Hospital came into being in 1922 on the transfer of the Galway Hospital (Infirmary) facilities from what was later the County buildings to the old workhouse site on Newcastle Road. The Central Hospital building was demolished in 1956 and was replaced by the Regional Hospital, now University College Hospital, Galway. (Courtesy Tom Kenny)

Happiest Days

The faces tell it all as the entire class is brought together in just two rows of desks for that famous photo shot. Taken in the 1950s, this photograph captures the happy break in class routine in the former Convent of Mercy National School in Francis Street. Bags and satchels lie scattered on the floor in the mad scramble for places as Sr Bridget looks on approvingly. (Courtesy Farrell's PhotoStudio)

1960s

Glenarde House

Glenarde House on Taylor's Hill, was a former home of the Persse family, proprietors of one of Galway's most famous distilleries. The building was constructed *c*.1840 and later came into the possession of the Boland (of biscuit fame) family in 1922. It was subsequently purchased by Paddy and Breda Ryan in 1961 and developed as the Ardilaun House Hotel. (Courtesy Paddy Ryan)

Interior of Glenarde House

Our picture shows the sitting-room of Glenarde heavy with rich turquoise wall papers, spilling brocades of golden curtains and 'love chairs', all recalling a former Victorian era when croquet and afternoon tea was the order of the day. (Courtesy Paddy Ryan)

Van Collection

The fleet of vans of wholesale distributor Frank Quinn are lined up for inspection beside his home in College Road in this 1960s photograph. Frank initially worked for the Northlight Razor Blade Company, driving once a week to Dublin for such supplies as blades, knicker elastic and combs. He started out on his own in the 1940s, but his business ceased with the arrival of the multinationals in the 1980s. Frank had nineteen children, one of whom, Martin, was subsequently Mayor of Galway in 2000. (Courtesy Martin Quinn)

President Kennedy

Great excitement is evident among the populace of Galway as the President of the United States, John F. Kennedy, is escorted by a Garda motorcycle guard of honour through Forster Street on his way to Eyre Square where he was made a Freeman of the city. Crowds gather outside Rabbitte's and Greaney's pubs to welcome Galway's most famous visitor on this never-to-be-forgotten day in 1963. The Magdalen complex forms a rather dour background to the jubilant scene. (Copyright *Connacht Tribune*)

Rod Licence Protest

Boats gather at the start of the annual Bráithreacht na Coiribe angling competition on the River Corrib at Woodquay in April 1966, with anglers displaying placards protesting at the end of free fishing, should impending government legislation be enacted. It would take another thirty-two years before this licence became law, with disastrous results. The former Clifden railway pillars stretch across the river to the Corrib Rowing and Yachting clubhouse, with the 19th-century Persse bonded whiskey store further to the left. Beyond, a crane signals the start of the expansion of the university campus. (Copyright *Connacht Tribune*)

Bottoms Up!

Down by Long Walk, a youngster leans over the stern of one of the derelict wooden trawlers, which originally brought ruin to the old Claddagh hookers due to the effectiveness of trawling as distinct from drift netting for herring or long-lining for other species. This trawler, and the remains of others, were later brought to Hare Island where they now moulder into history. The Quay Stream is in full flow, dividing Long Walk from the binary-coloured houses of the New Claddagh.

Donkey Transport
Michael Trayers, on his way in from Barna to the fowl and vegetable market at the Church of St Nicholas, gladly gives a spin on his cart to Maeve and Valerie Hession of St Joseph's Avenue. Mollie Hession, the girls' grandaunt, looks on. (Courtesy Christy Hession)

Angling Cup Winners
After the competition, Bráithreacht na Coiribe anglers gather around the various cups and trophies to be distributed to the winners at the annual dinner of the club in the former Galway Bay Hotel. Standing (*left to right*): Paddy Molloy, Jerry Flaherty, Frank Hynes, French Semple, Joe Lardner (hon. sec.), Jimmy Maloney, Michael O'Donnell, John Bartley, Frank Gallagher, Canon George Quinn (chaplin), Larry Wynne, Bartley Hehir, Mattie Hynes, — , Neil Boyle. Seated (*left to right*): — , Tom Tierney (Mayor) and Paddy Mulvehill (chairman). (Courtesy James Casserly and copyright *Connacht Tribune*)

Gaol Road

Gaol Road as it looked shortly after the Cathedral opened. To the right the overgrown foundations of the former gaol warders' houses await development into the delightful little waterside park that is there today. Further down, the former McDonogh store would be enlarged to house the reference section of County Galway Library as well as the County Vocational Education offices. In the background stands McDonogh's and Palmer's Mills, while the Poor Clare Convent is to the right beyond the Gaol, now Cathedral, River. (Courtesy Yann Studios)

Mud Dock

The 18th-century Eyre Mud Dock, which in later times was used only as a depository for decaying trawlers, suddenly saw service again when the coaster, *Karel*, berthed there in the late 1960s for repairs. She was probably the largest vessel ever to berth in this old dock area.

Aircraft Engine

Strange as it was to have a ship the size of the *Karel* berthed in the Mud Dock, even more unusual was the aircraft engine pictured on the pier beside the vessel. Dredged up by a trawler in Galway Bay, this engine came from an RAF aircraft which crashed there during World War II.

Liam Mellows Winners

Galway city's most famous hurling club, Liam Mellows, winners of the County final in 1968 after defeating Ardrahan in the old Pearse Stadium, Salthill. Back (*left to right*): Joe Casey, Paddy Ryan, Mick Lally, Pat Larkin, Ray Gilmore, Paddy Murphy, Bernard Diviney, Paddy Reilly. Front (*left to right*): Eoghan O'Sullivan, Lorcan O'Rourke, Jimmy Duggan, Gerry Mahony, Willie Concannon, Tony O'Connor, Jim Bishop. (Courtesy James Casserly)

'Shoots' Tuite

One of Galway's best-known characters was 'Shoots', as this genial Dubliner (or was he from Wicklow?) came to be known from his custom of 'shooting' everyone he met on the street or in cinemas, where he delighted in the 'cowboy' genre. His guns were two twigs which he carried in his belt or, in an emergency, he would use his pipe to rid the streets of 'bad lads' — he, naturally, was one of the 'good lads'. Visitors especially were fair game to this schoolboy who never quite grew up! (Courtesy Stan Sheilds and copyright *Connacht Tribune*)

'Swinging Sixties'

Galway, like everywhere else, rocked and rolled to the sound of the beat. Pictured here in red jackets with black velvet collars and in full swing are the Galway Blazers on a gig in the Warwick Hotel. George Herterich, Galway's recently retired and most famous victualler, is in full voice flanked by Willie O'Dowd (*left*) and Christy Donnelly (*right*) on electric guitars, with Billie Barrett on the drums. Sitting in front is 'Tex' Callaghan, manager of the group, enjoying the sound with the best of them.

Golf Club Captains

Galway Golf Club, founded in 1895, celebrated its centenary in some style in 1995. Hundreds of native and non-native Galwegians contributed to its success down through the years, including those past captains photographed here in 1965. (Copyright *Connacht Tribune*)

Jesuit Centenary

The year 1963 was a happy one in the history of the Jesuits in Galway when the Society celebrated the centenary of its presence there in October of that year. Our picture shows the congregation at the ceremonies in the packed Jesuit Church. (Copyright *Connacht Tribune*)

Busy Williamsgate Street

Except for buses, practically every means of transport is visible in this photograph of a rather busy Williamsgate Street in the 1960s. Despite the advances in motor transport, there was still room for the humble horse and cart, while the sun seemed to shine every day as is evident by the outstretched window shades on the left side of the street. (Copyright *Connacht Tribune*)

Opening of Mercy Secondary School

The Mercy Sisters, who first came to Galway in 1840, celebrated a great moment in their history with the opening of their secondary school in May 1967, at Newtownsmyth. Excited student participants in the ceremonies on the day are pictured here lined up outside their new school, as they await the arrival of the various clerical dignitaries. (Copyright *Connacht Tribune*)

Presentation Lilac Time

Presentation Convent, like other Galway centres of education, delighted in putting on various musical shows each year. Here are pictured those who starred in the show, *Lilac Time*, which was the school's selection for October 1963. (Copyright *Connacht Tribune*)

Lough Atalia Carnival

People, currachs and speedboats gather on the shoreline of Lough Atalia on 25 June 1965 during the once popular Lough Atalia Carnival. The event was mostly water-based with all sorts of craft events including currachs, outriggers and speedboats participating in competitive events. (Copyright *Connacht Tribune*)

Staff Dinner and Dance

With the economy gradually improving in the 1960s, new employment opportunities became available to Galwegians. One of the most exciting was the opening of a branch of the Woolworth chain of shops where Supermac's is today on Eyre Square. Like other such businesses, an added bonus was the annual staff dinner dance. Woolworth's employees are enjoying one in this photograph, which has the later famous Pat Quinn, assistant manager, sitting left, and Clarence Quinn of College Road, trainee manager, sitting right, on the staircase of the Great Southern Hotel. (Courtesy Owen Quinn)

Hession School of Dancing

Traditional Irish dancing has played an important part in the cultural life of Galway city. Various schools of dancing have operated in the city during the 20th century, with the most successful being the Celene Hession and Peggy Carty Schools of Dancing. Celene is pictured here with some of her successful charges in June 1967 as they show off their trophies. (Copyright *Connacht Tribune*)

Our Lady's Boys' Club (Rugby)

Rugby is another outdoor sport of Our Lady's Boys' Club which was founded in 1941 by Fr Leonard Shiel SJ, for the benefit of the city youth. Here we picture the club's Connacht Junior Cup finalists for 1965. Standing (*left to right*): Patsy (Durcan) Forde, Bartley Nolan, Noel Fay, Miceál Casserly, Owen Horan, David Cronin, Stephen Griffin, Michael Casserly and Dr Malcolm Little (referee). Front (*left to right*): Michael Grealish, Jimmy Cunningham, Murt Folan, Tom Burke, Tom Connell, Tom Keady, Brian Cassidy. (Courtesy James Casserly and copyright *Connacht Tribune*)

Harbour Development Scheme

Peter Cloherty is pictured rowing across the Commercial Dock towards the huge circular gasometer prior to the major harbour development scheme which commenced in 1963. The main change was the linking of the Commercial and the Dun Aengus Docks, and the closing of the entrance to the former. While working on the spoil removal to an area beyond Hare Island, Peter is said to have discovered an unrecorded rock shoal, which now bears the title, Peter Rock, in Admiralty charts! (Courtesy Peter Cloherty)

Black Box

A last look back from Wolfe Tone Bridge at the old 'Black Box', the former McDonogh fertiliser production factory, which closed down in 1969. At one time in the early 1930s it is said that 'half of Galway worked in McDonogh's and the other half wished they did'. Máirtín Mór McDonogh, who died in 1934, was responsible for the erection of this facility and many more in the city during the early part of the 20th century. (Courtesy McDonogh & Sons)

Cardinal Marella

Religious fervour reached a high level in 1961 when Cardinal Marella was made a Freeman of Galway. Our photograph shows the huge procession in his honour coming down Shop Street. Here we see members of the university followed by military officers. Next come Galway's famous Sword and Mace carried by fire officers. Then comes the mayor, Mr James Redington, followed by the city councillors. The clergy come next, with the cardinal in the place of honour at the rear. (Copyright *Connacht Tribune*)

Cathedral Cross

Clergy participate in the blessing of the great bronze cross, which shortly afterwards was raised and placed on the top of the dome of Galway's new cathedral. From the left are: Canon McDonogh, Canon Quinn, Canon Glynn, Canon Mitchell, Canon Spellman and Canon Hyland. The young server on the right is now Fr Des Forde. (Copyright *Connacht Tribune*)

Galway Race Fever
There is racing fever in the air as the horses thunder past the grandstand on the first circuit of the Galway Plate in a typical Galway Races scene of the 1960s. Shirt sleeves and blouses are evident in the summer weather as racegoers throng both levels of the old grandstand, while others pack the railings to get a close-up of their favourites. The stand is gone now, but memories of its glorious race days linger more than most. (Courtesy Jack Mahon and Galway Races' Committee)

The Tally Men
One of the most exciting aspects of the Irish political election process is the counting of the votes. As this process is soon to be entirely computerised, one will see the end of the 'tally men', those political stalwarts who watched each count and gave their verdict, usually correct, before the official one was announced. They are pictured here at work in an election count in Galway. (Copyright *Connacht Tribune*)

City's First Supermarket
Crowds gather outside the GTM in Shop Street, the city's first supermarket, to experience a new thrill in the shopping experience. Other indications from this photograph that the local economy was changing for the better include a packed double-decker bus making its way to sunny Salthill, while the 'Merc' speaks for itself. (Courtesy Tom Holohan)

Religious Processions
While the Corpus Christi religious procession was the largest held annually in the city, individual parishes also held their own processions from time to time. Here in the 1960s is pictured the Franciscan version winding its way along by the former St Brendan's National School, Woodquay, with the County Buildings in the background, and turning down Corrib Terrace. Jimmy Francis is pictured holding the Third Order banner. (Courtesy Farrell's PhotoStudio)

Newcastle House

Also known as Distillery House and the 'Tea House', this two-storeyed, cream-coloured building may have been built in the late 18th century on the banks of the River Corrib at Newcastle by the Persse family, whose first major distillery was built directly behind the building. A drum tower from the extensive garden still stands in the university grounds, while the tail race from the distillery runs through the college campus. The last occupants, the O'Hallorans, sold the property to the university in 1968 and the house was demolished in 1974. (Courtesy Angela McManus née O'Halloran)

Cathedral Ordinations

The joint ordination of four classmates of St Mary's College, Galway, was a happy event. It took place in Galway Cathedral on 19 June 1966. These were the first ordinations in the new cathedral. Posing for famous Galway photographer, Jimmy Walshe, are (*from the left*): Fr Patrick Callanan, Fr Michael Crosby, Bishop Michael Browne, Fr Frank Larkin and Fr Malachy Hallinan. Fr Crosby's other two brothers, Edward and Denis, also serve as priests in the Galway Diocese. (Courtesy Galway Diocesan Archives)

Opening of Galway Cathedral

A major milestone in the ecclesiastical history of Galway was the opening of Galway Cathedral on 15 August 1965 on the former jail site. Cardinal Cushing of Boston preached a sermon, 'Why Build a Cathedral?' during the Mass, while President Éamon de Valera lit the sanctuary lamp on this auspicious day for Catholicism in the city. As well as the Cardinal, four Archbishops accompanied Bishop Michael Browne on the altar. At the Consecration, the No. 1 Army Band played a fanfare 'which echoed throughout Ireland'. (Courtesy Galway Diocesan Archives)

Hurricane Debbie

Not since the 'Night of the Big Wind' on 6 January 1839, did Galway city experience such a natural disaster as occurred on 16 September 1961. Much damage was caused throughout the city. Parts of the River Corrib became practically dry while the storm raged. Pictured here is a tree blown down between the Courthouse and the Salmon Weir Bridge. (Copyright *Connacht Tribune*)

Packed Salthill

Every picture tells a story and this one of a packed beach in June 1963 reflects the long, hot summers of not so long ago. In the background one can see the end of the 'green belt' with one of its large houses. In the middle is the Hanger, Galway's favourite dancing spot during the 1930s, while a newly painted Eglinton Hotel can be seen on the right. (Copyright *Connacht Tribune*)

'West Awake'

Pictured here in the late 1960s are the participants in the West United Soccer Club's Past Versus Present Team Competition, which was held in the old Terryland Park. Back (*from left*): Joe Philbin, Joe Keady, Tommy Murphy, Martin Turke, Frank Donoghue, Paddy Byrne, Don Deacy, Pat O'Donnell, Billy Murray, Paul Fallon, Tommy Lee, Christy Hession and Tommy Hynes. Front (*from left*): Tom Murray, Seán Boyle, Seán Lally, Frank Murphy, Eamon Howley, Peter Mernagh, James O'Toole, Ollie Walsh, Michael Murphy, Eamon Deacy, John Flannery and Michael Connor. Mascots: — and Derek O'Connor. (Courtesy Christy Hession)

Potez Ship

Not too long ago Galway Docks were much busier than they are today. Pictured here in June 1963 is a ship loading heaters for export from Potez, the new factory at Mervue. Nine dockers, it seems, await the lifting of more heaters from the CIE lorry parked on the right! (Copyright *Connacht Tribune*)

Opening of Potez

A very important day in the industrial history of Galway occurred in June 1963 when the Taoiseach, Mr Seán Lemass, opened the major Potez complex in Mervue. It manufactured huge quantities of gas fires which were exported all over the world. (Copyright *Connacht Tribune*)

Empty Docks

Two workmen (where would Galway be without them?) are dwarfed by the high walls of the empty docks during the 1960s development, which saw the Commercial and Dún Aengus Docks united in the biggest harbour scheme since the former was completed in 1840. The retaining wall, containing the harbour offices and spur railway line, was removed and the entrance gates to the Commercial Dock (behind the men) blocked up in one of the biggest construction schemes in Galway's history. (Copyright *Connacht Tribune*)

1970s

Passenger Shed

Hopes of a renewed transatlantic passenger liner trade were renewed in Galway as one of the city's first giant construction cranes towers over the main dock pier during the building of a passenger transit shed. Alongside are berthed many of the old wooden trawlers which made up the Galway fishing fleet at the time, prior to the advent of new steel-hulled vessels and their subsequent departure to Rossaveel, which became the main fishing port for Connacht.

Fowl Market

There was much more activity at the Saturday fowl and vegetable market beside the Church of St Nicholas when this photograph was taken just a few days before Christmas. Geese and turkeys were now on sale, and there are many more people crowded into the narrow streets seeking Christmas dinner at a bargain price. The garda in the distance is having difficulty making way for the car going away from the photographer. (Copyright *Connacht Tribune*)

Memorial Headstone

The Mayor of Galway, Miceál Ó h-Uiginn, unveiling in September 1972 a memorial headstone in St James's Cemetery, Mervue, on the grave of Sean Mulvoy of College Road, a Volunteer killed in action at the railway station by Crown Forces on 8 September 1920. Pictured also in attendance are historian Rev. Martin Coen, and those who held the mayoral office including Gerry Colgan, Paddy Flaherty, Bridie O'Flaherty and Brendan Holland. (Courtesy Michael McHugh)

Political Rally

The 'real Taoiseach', Jack Lynch TD, speaks in Eyre Square to Fianna Fáil faithful including Prof. T.P. O'Neill with pipe (left of iron pole), while directly in front of him, with hat, Matt Hackett listens with great interest, as does Freda Nee (*front left*). Some of the 'unfaithful' are present also, as is evident from posters protesting against the speaker's policies on Northern Ireland and the European Economic Community. (Copyright *Connacht Tribune*)

Galway on Fire

The Great Galway Fire of 1971 started in the timber section of McDonogh Merchants on Merchants' Road on the morning of 20 August. By the time the fire brigade arrived, the firm's timber and coal yards were both ablaze. Fanned by a strong breeze, the fire quickly engulfed the adjacent Corbett's timber yard and eventually Corbett's shop, pictured here on Williamsgate Street. A six acre inner city block was destroyed with over £2 million worth of damage sustained in what was described as Galway's greatest natural disaster. (Copyright *Connacht Tribune*)

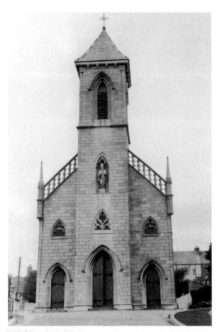

Old Church

The former St Patrick's Church, Forster Street, closes its door to church services in 1972. This fine cut stone building was officially opened on 11 January 1842. Its foundation stone was laid on 17 May 1836, but before the building was completed its roof was blown off on the 'Night of the Big Wind', 6 January 1839. The adjacent new St Patrick's was opened on 30 July 1972.

Cathedral Carpark

A rather empty Galway Cathedral carpark greets the visitor on this day in the late 1970s. To the right is the administration section of the cathedral, while in the distance the large building, formerly Regan's, then Cloran's and eventually McDonogh's flour mill, would soon be purchased to house various sections of the Engineering Department of the university. The new (1972) Hygeia office block is in the left background, while the stone store to the right would soon be restored to house VEC and County Galway library facilities. (Courtesy Yann Studios)

Kirwan's Lane

One of Galway's oldest lanes, named after the Kirwans, lies derelict and full of memories in this 1970s' picture. John Kirwan's house, at the top of the lane on the left, was once home to the Dominican (1686) and Presentation (1815) nuns, and is now the popular Busker Browne's pub. The plaque over the medieval stone doorway (left foreground) records that Wolfe Tone, the famous Irish martyr, once 'trod the boards' with Humanity Dick Martyn's wife in Galway's first theatre here in the 18th century. The laneway has since been greatly restored.

Quiet Backwater

A rather lonely Whitehall in the late 1970s. The little row of terraced houses on the left (one was home to the famous local singer, Ned Joyce) would in time make way for modern social housing. The back entrance to Corbett's shop as well as the stores and garages on the right would become the site of the Edward Square and Eyre Square Shopping Centres. The large gabled building with chimney in the distance was the 18th-century hospital attached to the Citadel Military Barracks.

Silent Streets

The end of the 1970s saw depression on the empty streets of Galway as is evident here where Cross, Flood and St Augustine Streets meet. Crumbling buildings and cleared medieval sites greet the eye. It would be many years before Designated Areas and a Celtic Tiger would breathe life back into streets once noisy with the bustle of commerce based mainly on a Continental wine trade, which saw Galway port 'second only to London and Bristol' in these islands. Those who decry modern Galway might well dwell a little on this photograph!

'Banners' Murphy

Known as one of the most versatile anglers in the city, William 'Banners' Murphy is pictured in the 1970s sitting on a fish box watched by admiring fans. Two innovations are discernible. One of the first plastic bags seen in Galway now encloses his catch, while 'Banners' demonstrates the advantages of the new 'glass' rod in his pursuit of mackerel. The dock gates were another place from which to fish, while in the background stands the one-storey Harbour Office with adjacent railway line, both of which were removed in later harbour improvements.

Fishery Tower

The end of an era as the Galway Fishery ceases to be a private concern and becomes a state-owned asset at the end of the 1970s. Consequently, the former Fishery Tower at Wolfe Tone Bridge lies derelict when the state ceased the salmon netting operations carried out from this building since the 1860s. In more recent times, the Galway Civic Trust has restored this unique building and has developed it as a fishery museum, the only one of its type in Ireland.

Clybaun Mill

The start of a new milling process in Galway's early history was revealed during the 1970s with the discovery of the remains of a horizontal mill in the little stream at Clybaun. The wooden frame of the former building and water chute gave a carbon date of c.600 A.D. The stream and find site are now covered by housing developments on the western side of the city. (Courtesy Archaeology Dept, NUI, Galway)

Railway Retirement

Always sad and yet a happy event, retiring from work needs to be recorded. This was certainly done in style for train examiner, Tommy Smullen, who retired from CIE in 1971. Pictured celebrating the event are front (*left to right*): Tom Feeney, Paddy Egan, Joe Walsh and Michael O'Halloran. Back (*left to right*): Jim Crowley, Christy Roche, — , Tommy Smullen, Tom Clancy, Bobbie Healy, Johnny Flaherty, John Foy, Jim Ward, John Noone, Jim Sheridan, Tom Murphy, Michael Ward and Martin Quinn (later Mayor of Galway). (Courtesy Martin Quinn)

Naomh Éanna

A lone angler standing on the Dock Pier views the Aran tender, *Naomh Éanna*, as she heads into Galway Docks laden mostly with day-trippers from the Aran Islands. A caravan and car can also be seen on the upper deck of a ship that now acts as a maritime museum in Dublin. The tender first came to Galway on 5 May 1958 and was decommissioned in 1988.

Technical School Win

Pictured here in 1973 are the All-Ireland Senior Project winners from Fr Griffin Road Technical School, now the Galway Technical Institute. With teacher Seamus Ó Scannlain are group leader Joseph Conroy, John Flaherty, Mary Bermingham, Michael Curran, Rita Conneely and Bernadette Madden. Their study project, entitled 'The Oyster Farmers of Galway Bay', was judged by the Irish Productivity Centre to be the best from 400 second-level school entries. (Courtesy GTI)

Open Air Concert

Galway city has always been syonymous with *ceol agus craic* as is evidenced in this open air concert which was held in Eyre Square in 1971 in aid of Northern Ireland refugees. A well-known character, Máirtín 'Mate' Lydon, is pictured in full swing in the two-hand reel, with the music supplied by the famous Ceoltóirí Chonnacht. (Courtesy Jack Cunningham)

Badminton Win

In 1974, after a break of many years, a Galway city team represented by the Columban Badminton Club won Senior and Junior County championships, beating Headford in both finals. Seated (*left to right*): Jennifer Taylor, Betty Ferguson, Lenor Campbell, Julie Nolan and Mary Langan. Standing (*left to right*): Bert Flaherty, Tom O'Neill, Peadar O'Dowd and Padraic McNally. (Copyright *Connacht Tribune*)

Franciscan Celebration
Friends and colleagues gather around Cletus Noone OFM celebrating the Silver Jubilee of his ordination and present him with a cake in the shape of the Abbey Church by confectioner, Frank Hynes. Included are Bridie Grealish, Frances Duffy, Fr Colohan, Maura Noone, M. Grealish, Bishop Eamon Casey, Fr Rabbitte, Fr Noone, Rita Waters, Mary O'Donnell, Fr Des O'Malley, Fr Hillary, Fr Ralph Lawless and Brother Declan. (Courtesy Frank Hynes)

Library Change
The end of an era in the life of UCG came in 1973 when the original college library closed and the James Hardiman Library opened in its new building. Staff involved in the changeover are pictured here with librarian Christy Townley standing in the right foreground. (Courtesy NUI, Galway)

Moon's Corner Congestion

Even back in the late 1970s Moon's Corner had its share of traffic. Pictured here is the Salthill double-decker bus almost clipping the tail light off a Post Office van driven by Ned Conneely from Bohermore as it drives into the Post Office depot entrance beside Matt O'Flaherty's pharmacy. Meanwhile, the unfortunate cyclist still had problems negotiating Galway's busiest corner. (Copyright *Connacht Tribune*)

'Ladneen' Curran

Appropriately, the 'king to be' of the Claddagh is pictured here in March 1973, sitting amidst the paraphernalia of the sea, with Quay Stream in the background. Paddy 'Ladneen' Curran succeeded Martin Oliver as king in August of that year and served the Claddagh with distinction until his death in July 1993. Happily, the tradition of the king is alive and well in the Claddagh today, with Michael Lynskey playing the role to perfection. (Copyright *Connacht Tribune*)

New Regional Technical College

Séamus MacDomhnaill, CEO of the City of Galway VEC (*left*), greets and invites Richard Burke, Minister for Education (*centre*), to officially open the Regional Technical College, Galway, on 12 April 1973. On the right is Gay Corr, Principal and later Director of the Galway-Mayo Institute of Technology, which replaced the RTC. Mr Corr acted as head of this third-level institution for twenty-nine years, thus becoming one of the city's leading academics of all time. (Courtesy Bernard O'Hara)

Come Blow Your Horn
One of the funniest comedies ever staged at the Taibhdhearc was *Sín do Sciathán* (Come Blow Your Horn) by Neil Simon, which ran from 20 to 27 February 1977. Directed by Máire Stafford, the cast, as shown in this photograph, included those holding hands, Muireann Ní Bhrolcháin and Pat Heaney, while showing a little more than angst at the back are Mairéad Ní Nuadháin and Seán Stafford. (Courtesy Seán Stafford)

Teaghlach Bhernarda Alba
Comh maith le Siobhán McKenna, bean eile atá dlú bhaint aice leis an Taibhdhearch ná Máire Stafford. Leis a fhear chéile, Seán, tá Máire ag obair ins an amharclainn spéisialta seo ar feadh 40 blianta mar aisteoir agus stiúirthóir. Ins an dráma seo, *Teaghlach Bhernard Alba* san Taibhdhearc i 1976, tá sí ina suí ar chlé in éinde le Muireann Ní Bhrolcháin, Máiread Ní Choinceanainn, Nóra Ní Anrachtaigh, Máiread Ní Nuadháin, Colette Ní Éanaigh, agus Loretta Ní Cheallaigh. (Courtesy Seán Stafford)

Keeping the Old Tradition
'Blessing the Bay', one of the oldest traditions in the Claddagh, is personified in this happy photograph of Eileen Cloherty (*left*) and Molly Browne 'on their beads' as they answer the Dominican priest on board a mixed flotilla of boats from the Claddagh. The boats have gathered in a circle off Mutton Island in the time-honoured custom to ask God's blessing for a bountiful harvest from the sea. (Courtesy Joe Shaughnessy and copyright *Connacht Tribune*)

St Patrick's Day Parade

One of the first modern floats to make its appearance in the annual St Patrick's Day Parade featured the Bunratty performers on the CIE entry as they publicised the tourist delights of the West. Ann Melia is pictured holding the large 'harp' as the float moves through the top of Eyre Square with Woolworth's in the background. (Courtesy Martin Quinn)

Methodist Church

Now used for combined services of the Methodist and Presbyterian congregations in Galway, the Methodist Church on Queen Street is a Galway landmark since its erection *c*.1835. Incorporated into the one facade of squared blocks of native limestone is the schoolhouse reached by an exterior staircase. On the left can be seen a portion of the former CIE premises, now replaced by the Victoria Hotel.

Corrib Finds

In the late 1970s, while retrieving an outboard engine from the bed of the River Corrib at Woodquay, divers found a 17th-century sword lying nearby. Subsequent searches of the entire river bed over the next few years uncovered many artefacts dating from the Stone Age up to the present time. Pictured here are divers Noel Higgins, Patsy Griffin and Brendan Mulligan with some of the first finds.

The Pope in Ballybrit

Who will ever forget that marvellous day, 30 September 1979, when Pope John Paul II came to say Mass for the youth of Ireland in the vast expanse of Ballybrit Race Course? 'Young people of Ireland, I love you' was his famous declaration to the vast congregation, the largest gathering of people ever recorded in the city. (Courtesy Galway Diocesan Archives)